STREAMS OF HISTORY
THE UNITED STATES

STREAMS OF HISTORY
THE UNITED STATES

BY

ELLWOOD W. KEMP

EDITED BY

LISA M. RIPPERTON

YESTERDAY'S CLASSICS

CHAPEL HILL, NORTH CAROLINA

This edition, first published in 2008 by Yesterday's Classics, an imprint of Yesterday's Classics, LLC, is an edited excerpt from a work originally published by Ginn and Company in 1902. For the complete listing of the books that are published by Yesterday's Classics, please visit www.yesterdaysclassics.com. Yesterday's Classics is the publishing arm of the Baldwin Online Children's Literature Project which presents the complete text of hundreds of classic books for children at www.mainlesson.com.

ISBN-10: 1-59915-260-6

ISBN-13: 978-1-59915-260-8

Yesterday's Classics, LLC
PO Box 3418
Chapel Hill, NC 27515

CONTENTS

THE DEVELOPMENT OF THE NATION

1789–1902

WE have now come to a time when the American people began to live under a form of government in some particulars different from any ever worked out before. This was a federal government, providing for two great things: first, for a strong independent central power deriving its authority from the people; and second, for strong local or state governments, likewise deriving their powers from the people. It was thus the desire of the framers of the Constitution to form a government in which the states should work harmoniously with the central government, like many little cogwheels working in one great central wheel. Although we found the English government to be the freest and best developed in Modern Europe, yet, in the hands of a selfish king like George III, the self-reliant Anglo-Saxon living in America found it impossible to live under it and enjoy the freedom he was determined to have. The central power under the English king grew too strong, and hence, as we have seen, the Americans declared themselves independent, manfully gained their independence in the war of the Revolution, soon after formed the Articles of Confederation, hoping thereby to form a government in which a few could not secure supreme control at the expense of the liberties of the many. But, as we have seen in the sixth volume of this series, in less than ten years of trial of the Articles, they were found insufficient to give the Americans a vital, permanent nation, able to tax its citizens and control and guarantee the liberties of its people; for, from fear of too strong a central government, the framers of the Articles had gone too far toward the opposite extreme and had placed the real power in the hands of the states, leaving the central government "no stronger than a rope of sand."

From this experience came the Constitution of 1789. The Articles had kept the idea of American nationality alive in the minds of the people, and had bridged over the interval of slow national growth till it was possible to form a government in which there should be an equal balance between state and nation, and in which the people might have opportunity to develop the greatest possible liberty. The work before us now consists in following the developing national life of the American people and in seeing whether the Constitution proved to be what was claimed for it. Has it made of the American people one great free nation, instead of a number of jealous independent states?

First let us look at the extent of our country in 1789. It consisted of thirteen states stretching along the Atlantic coast from the territory of Florida, which at that time belonged to Spain, to the line dividing Maine from Canada, and included the great stretch of territory extending westward from these states to the

Mississippi River. It was by and for the people living in these lands that the Constitution was written and ratified. It was founded upon an agreement between the people and was itself the fundamental law by which they were to be governed,—in other words, a set of rules ordained and established by themselves as the source of authority and to which they must yield obedience; and henceforth, when any question of law should arise, they would, through their officers, turn to these rules to decide what to do.

The United States became a nation under the Constitution in 1788, nine states having ratified it; and in the following year, on April 30, 1789, General Washington was inaugurated first President of the Republic. Every one knew how much he had done to gain the independence of the colonies and to cement them into a strong nation; so it was natural that the universal desire should have been to have such an unselfish patriot placed at the head of affairs to set the new governmental machinery going. At the end of his first term (1793) he was again chosen President. By this time, however, political parties were arising. Let us see how this came about.

There were many who opposed the ratification of the Constitution when it was placed before the conventions in the several states, because they thought it gave the central government too much power. Now that the Constitution had been adopted, they set about to hold as strictly to its provisions as possible. These were called Strict Constructionists. Those who had favored and worked for the Constitution, wanted to give the central, or Federal, government a great deal of power; that is, they desired to interpret the provisions of the Constitution in such a way as to give authority for the central government to do much toward regulating commerce, establishing banks, building roads, imposing a protective tariff and the like. These were called Broad Constructionists.

Of course, what the Constitution did or did not allow was a matter to be decided in the first place by the Congress and executive officers in the regular performance of their work, but finally by the Supreme Court. Thus there came to be two parties in the United States: those who were in favor of a strong Federal, or central, government, who took the name of Federalists, and those who were opposed to a strong central government, who until 1792 called themselves Anti-Federalists. Although the rise of these parties began during Washington's terms of office, the principles which they advocated were not clearly set off till after his last term, for Washington held all the people well together and made up his Cabinet of advisers from men of both parties.

First, he chose as Secretary of State, Thomas Jefferson, the writer of the Declaration of Independence and now the leader of the Anti-Federalist party. For Secretary of the Treasury he chose Alexander Hamilton, as ardent a Federalist as Jefferson was an Anti-Federalist. Besides these, he appointed Henry Knox, a Federalist, Secretary of War, and Edmund Randolph, an Anti-Federalist, Attorney-General. Thus Washington's first Cabinet was composed of two Federalists and two Anti-Federalists. With these especial advisers in each department of the government, Washington put in motion the national government under our present Constitution.

There were many trying questions which came up during Washington's first term which required great insight and wisdom for settlement. One of the most perplexing difficulties was the providing of means for paying old debts contracted during the Confederacy, and for paying the running expenses of the government. This was given to Hamilton to work out and to report his plan to Congress. Hamilton, as already said, was Secretary of the Treasury. He had from the first been one of the strongest supporters of the Constitution, and now began to put life into it by showing the entire country how quickly he could raise taxes under it to pay the outstanding debts of the country.

Besides our debts to France and other foreign countries, the government owed a great deal of money to Revolutionary soldiers, and others, who had lent it money to carry on the war. But the government had no money with which to pay debts, so Congress, by the advice of Hamilton, passed a law, taxing certain articles brought into and sold in the United States, and the money thus obtained was used to pay the national debt. In this way a tariff, designed mainly for revenue, arose. Different articles, such as wine, silk, tea, sugar, etc., were taxed when they were shipped into the country, and the money obtained was turned into the United States Treasury. But the government had also another way of raising money. Besides the tax on foreign goods brought into the United States, taxes were laid on certain articles made in the United States, as, for example, so many cents per gallon on whisky. This was called an internal revenue tax, because it was placed on articles made in our own country for home consumption. This tax was resisted in 1793 by persons who were distilling liquors in western Pennsylvania, but it was forcibly collected by government officers. By examples like these, you can see how much stronger and firmer is the hand of the general government under the Constitution, in all these money matters, than it was under the Articles of Confederation. Millions of the national debt were paid during Washington's administrations through Hamilton's intelligent guidance of financial affairs.

Another question which Washington was called on to settle (1793) was what our relation should be with England and France. England and France were at this time at war with each other, and France asked the United States for help, while England, also, was equally desirous of getting our help. Now, although France had helped win American independence, and had still due her from the United States a large sum of money, Washington knew that for our infant Republic to engage then in foreign war would endanger the government itself. He thus refused help, issued a Proclamation of Neutrality as between France and England, but directed arrangements to be made at once by the Secretary of the Treasury for paying France what was due her. Here the strength of the new Republic was beginning to show itself in our successful and independent dealings with foreign nations.

It was during Washington's term also that the national bank was created, it being likewise a part of the financial plan of Hamilton. The capital of the bank was fixed at ten million dollars, of which the government owned two million, while the rest was held by the people. Hamilton saw that by leading the people to become interested in a national bank, they would also become interested in the national government which created the bank. This was not just one banking house, but a system of banks, with its center in Philadelphia, and sub-banks or branches in other cities. The number of banks grew, as the number and size of cities grew throughout the country. The collected revenue of the country was deposited in these banks, and they were to help the government in making payments to government officers, such as postmasters, army officers and soldiers, all over the United States. The charter, or law, regulating the bank was passed by Congress in 1791, for twenty years. It would thus have a right to do business till 1811, but no longer, unless Congress at that time should renew the charter. In 1792 a mint was established at Philadelphia, by the government, for the making of United States money of gold, silver and copper; and at the same time, our decimal system of ten mills make one cent, ten cents one dime, etc., was begun. By means of the bank money and the money made by the mint the country was supplied with the proper means of carrying on its growing business. Placing the entire money system under the control of the central government made it vastly superior to what it was under the Articles of Confederation, when each state exercised the power to make its own money. So far, things seem to be moving on well under the new Constitution. The people in general came slowly to have interest in the nation, as they saw it bringing peace, order and prosperity to them.

The fact was, the country was not only growing richer and more populous along the Atlantic coast, but it was extending its population into the West. The Constitution provides for the admission of new states into the Union by Congress. During the early years of the government three new states, Vermont (1791), Kentucky (1792), and Tennessee (1796) became members of the Union. This shows that there had been emigration westward. Our national life was seeking new territory in which to expand. From the time the first settlers stepped upon the eastern shore, almost two centuries before, they had slowly pushed westward. The most rapid progress was made in the northern and middle states. With their liberal ideas of institutions they took up the westward march. With ax and gun on shoulder, and the ideal of a free republic in heart and mind, they went forth into the Western wilderness to conquer the Indian and the forest, and to erect therein free states, free religions and free schools. It has been said that the entire history of the Anglo-Saxon race is that of an ever-increasing hunger for land. No country has furnished a better example of this than our own, for long before there were open roads westward, the farmers followed the hunter through the mountain passes, and built their cabins and planted their cornfields and tobacco patches in the wildernesses of Ohio, Kentucky and Tennessee. First came the frontiersmen, generally on pack horses, to the lands which struck their fancy. They built a blockhouse, without nails, to guard themselves from the Indians, cultivated the soil with rude tools, and lived by the products of rifle and hoe. This liberty-loving Teuton was repeating in America, with much the same tools, what he had done a thousand years before in conquering Europe. Later on came emigrants in wagons. The hardy New England pioneer, seeking a western home, would stop his horses or oxen in the wilderness, tumble out boxes and barrels, spade and ax, and set about building a rude shelter for his family and animals. This done, his next task was to clear the ground and prepare for his first crop. Very soon the church and log schoolhouse followed , and it was not long till the newspaper appeared to help break the monotony of his isolated life and shed some rays of light into his wilderness home.

Thus, you see, as the states on the Atlantic slope grew more populous the western territories were gradually being filled with lusty, vigorous Teutonic folk, and admitted to the Union on perfect equality with the old states. Although most of these settlers were rough, they took with them the ideas of organization. So strong is the American's disposition to organize and live in peace and order, that it has been said, if a number of Americans should be shipwrecked on an uninhabited island, the first thing they would do would be to hold a mass meeting and elect a chairman and secretary. It is not to be wondered at, then, that as rapidly as the wilderness fell before the ax of the frontiersman the statehouse, church, schoolhouse and printing press rose in his tracks.

At the close of his second term, in 1797, against the desire of the entire country, Washington retired to his home at Mt. Vernon, Virginia, where two years later he died. His successor, John Adams, had been Vice President during both of Washington's administrations. In the autumn of 1796 he was elected President by the Federalists over Jefferson, the leader of the Democratic-Republicans (as the Anti-Federalists were called from about 1792 to 1830). According to the Constitution at that time, the candidate for President receiving the second largest number of votes became Vice President. Jefferson thus became Vice President under Adams. Since that time, however, the Constitution has been changed so that the President and Vice President are voted for separately.

Adams served only one term, and his administration is marked mainly by the stand taken by Kentucky and Virginia in regard to some laws passed by Congress. The United States was having trouble with France and with England on the seas, and there were some Americans who wanted to bring on trouble with England by helping France, while others wished to help England against France. Because this help was not given they criticised Congress and the President, principally by writing articles in the newspapers. So sharply and bitterly did the Americans side with one nation or the other that a foreigner traveling in this country at that time said that he found here many Englishmen and many Frenchmen, but no Americans. To stop this criticism two laws were passed by Congress, called the Alien and Sedition laws. The first gave the President right to send out of the United States, without allowing him trial in court, any alien whom he thought dangerous to the country. You can easily see that such a law would give the President enormous power if he chose to exercise it. The sedition law provided for the punishment of any one who should speak, write or publish anything false or abusive of either the President or Congress. While the first law was never enforced, under the latter several persons were fined and one was imprisoned. Very many people believed these laws to be wrong, for the first Amendment to the Constitution declares that the government shall have no right to interfere with the freedom of speech or of the press. As the last law seemed to do so, it was said by many to be unconstitutional.

The people of Virginia and Kentucky went so far as to declare in their legislatures, that Congress, in passing these laws, had gone beyond the powers given to it by the people of the states when they formed the Constitution; that such legislation was consequently without authority; and that the people of these states, because of the powers reserved to them under the Constitution, would be justified in not submitting to these laws. They believed that each state for itself, and not the national Supreme Court, had a right to say when Congress had gone beyond its just powers. From this point of view the continuance of the Union would depend upon Congress exercising no power which the states individually believed to belong to themselves. Out of these ideas grew the doctrines of nullification and secession in later years. The alien and sedition laws were opposed by the Democratic-Republicans and by many of the Federalists; so, as soon as Jefferson, the great leader of the Democratic-Republican party, became President, in 1801, they were repealed,—that is, set aside by Congress. The Federalist party had now (1801) been in power twelve years, and had done great service in firmly establishing the national government at home, and giving it credit and dignity abroad. But the people, believing the Federalists were tending toward despotism in passing the alien and sedition laws, voted that party out, and the Democratic-Republicans became in 1801 the ruling party. They now, however, shortened their name to that of Republican party. So from this time, down to about 1825, this party was known as the Republican party, while the opposing one, down to 1815, was known as the Federal party.

When Washington became President the national capital was New York City. In 1790 the capital was removed to Philadelphia, where it remained until 1800, when it was changed to Washington. Many objected at that time to having it so far west, for they had no idea that the United States would ever spread to the west as it has. But in 1803 this narrow notion of national growth began to change when Jefferson, urged forward by the desires of the people who had settled the western wilderness, bought from France for fifteen million dollars the Louisiana Territory. By this purchase the United States secured all the territory between Texas and Canada and westward to the Rocky Mountains, an area of over six hundred million acres, at a cost of two and one-half cents per acre. It is interesting and important to note that this great leader of the Republicans, Jefferson, who had up to this time maintained that the general government should do nothing but what the Constitution said plainly in so many words it might do, here acted upon the theory of the Federalists rather than that of the party to which he belonged, since the Constitution nowhere says expressly that the general government may buy foreign land. The far-reaching effects of the purchase can hardly be appreciated, for it not only gave the people of the United States possession of the mouth of the Mississippi River, so that they could freely ship their western corn, wheat, pork, tobacco and cotton out to foreign countries, but it also gave them the western half of the Mississippi Valley,—so broad, fertile, abundantly watered, so rich in minerals and so temperate in climate as to lead the great Humboldt to call it "the noblest valley in the world."

There could have been no better time for such a purchase. The United States was again in trouble with France and England, both of which still continued the war with each other which had been going on most of the time for ten years; and since, as warring powers, they greatly interfered with our commerce by capturing our trading ships as they crossed the ocean, Congress passed a law, called an embargo, barring, as it were, our ships in their harbors and completely stopping for a time our trade with all foreign countries. This destroyed a great shipping industry which had sprung up on the Atlantic and threw many people out of employment. Thus, just at the time when the eastern door of commerce—the Atlantic Ocean—was closed to labor the western door to vast virgin fields was thrown open to invite laborers to cheap western lands. Already settlers dotted the wilderness back to the Mississippi, especially along the streams. These self-reliant people made their way down the western slope of the Appalachian Mountains into the valley of the Mississippi, and, as already said, soon came to have more grain and stock than they could themselves use. What every western farmer, land owner and townsman felt the need of was an outlet for his surplus crops. They could not haul their wheat and corn and pork and beef and wool from the Ohio and Mississippi valleys eastward, for there were as yet no good roads binding the great central valley to the Atlantic coast cities.

To meet this need came first the flatboat, and soon every stream was alive with boats bearing the western harvest down the current into the Mississippi and then down to New Orleans, from which port they made their way up to the Atlantic coast states, to the West Indies, and to countries across the sea. It was a long route, but the best that could be had until roads could be built from the Atlantic coast back westward over mountain and river, and through marsh and forest. The flatboat not only carried products out, but it brought thousands of settlers in. It had, however, one great disadvantage,— while it could with ease go down stream with the current, it was almost impossible for it to make way against the current and ascend the stream.

This difficulty began to be remedied in 1807, for in that year Robert Fulton first applied steam to a boat in such a way as to turn a large paddle wheel in the water and move the boat, even against the current. With this invention came other great migrations of emigrants from the East to the West. Within a short time steamboats began to appear on every important river; and now that Louisiana was a part of the national territory, boats began to push rapidly up the western rivers, carrying the hunter and trapper, the trader and farmer, and returned loaded with wheat, pork, tobacco, wool and corn.

Jefferson's two terms as President (1801–1809) covered a period of growth and prosperity, but our trouble with France and England, chiefly concerning commerce on the seas, had not yet been settled; so from the date when James Madison became President (1809) it was only three years until the United States was at war with England. We have seen how England and France, interfering with the commerce of the United States, had led Congress to pass the Embargo Act. In addition to seizing our ships at sea, England insisted upon the right to search American vessels for British sailors. Chiefly for these things the United States went to war with England in 1812. The war was opposed by the Federalists, especially by the shippers in New England, who found their remaining trade ruined and their seaport towns attacked by the British. But Madison and the Republican party kept up the war, and hoped to conquer Canada and annex it to the United States. An army was sent by Madison to undertake this, but the attempt ended in utter failure. Although unsuccessful on land, the Americans did better on the sea; and not alone there, they also won great naval victories on Lakes Erie and Champlain, and thus prevented the invasion of the United States from Canada by water. The war was brought to an end in 1815 by a treaty with England, but before the news could travel to America (there were no Atlantic cables then) a great victory on land was won by the Americans. The British attacked New Orleans, which was defended by Andrew Jackson with an army half the size of the British force. The English were very badly defeated and soon news of peace stopped further action.

Meanwhile, the New England Federalists (the chief shippers of the country) had grown dissatisfied, on account of the war stopping their shipbuilding and commerce; and having called a convention at Hartford, they framed in it some propositions, identical in spirit and principle with the Virginia and Kentucky Resolutions, which they desired to have passed as Amendments to the Constitution. They asked, among other things, to be allowed to defend themselves against attacks on their coast, and also to retain a portion of the Federal taxes for this purpose. Thus, the Federalists—the original strong central government party—were here opposing the actions of the central government, and seeking to enlarge the powers of the states. Some of the New England states have been accused, but probably unjustly, of having intentions of withdrawing from the Union at this time. However, before the delegates of the Hartford convention reached Washington to bring the propositions before Congress, peace between the United States and England was declared (1815).

While there seemed to be very little in the treaty of peace favorable to the United States, England never again attempted to interfere with American commerce or to search American vessels for seamen accused of deserting from the English naval service. The war had also another great influence: as it stopped New England shipping, for a time people turned to other means of making a living. With their great advantage of swift streams, giving unlimited power for turning wheels, New England was especially suited for carrying on manufacturing; hence mills sprang up there, and manufacturing rapidly became their leading industry.

As soon as the war was ended, and trade was resumed with England, English merchants began sending great quantities of manufactured goods to the United States. Being new in the work, and having to pay a higher price for labor than the English paid, the American manufacturer could not make goods as cheaply as the English; and as the English were thus enabled to undersell them, the Americans feared that their business would be ruined. To prevent this they sent representatives to Congress, who asked that a heavy tax be placed on imported goods, so that, by the time the English importers paid this tax they could not afford to sell so cheaply as the American makers could. As I have already said, manufacturing had grown greatly during the past few years, and seeing that this industry must be weakened, if not destroyed, unless a higher tariff were imposed, Congress consented to tax imported goods in order to protect the home industry. In this way arose the first protective tariff. As you have already seen, a tariff had been placed upon imported goods as early as Washington's first term, but it was a low tax, and mainly intended to raise revenue for the expense of the government. The tariff of 1816 had for its main purpose the protection of goods produced in our own country. Madison, having served two terms, retired to his landed estates at Montpellier, Virginia, and was succeeded by James Monroe, a Republican, who was also President for two terms (1817–1825). It was during this time that he and his able Secretary of State, John Quincy Adams, gave to America what is called the Monroe Doctrine. Spain's South American colonies having rebelled, Monroe warned the Holy Alliance, consisting of Russia, Prussia, Austria and France, from assisting Spain in reconquering her colonies. He said, while America was determined not to interfere with affairs abroad, she was equally determined to allow no interference by the Holy Alliance in American affairs; nor would the United States, he said, permit foreign nations to colonize any longer on the American continents. The Spanish colonies were driven to their struggle for liberty by Spain's despotic rule over them, and they were, no doubt, greatly stimulated to struggle for freedom by the example of free government which they saw developing so well in the United States.

So far we have said nothing of what was rapidly coming to be the most important question to the American nation, namely, the question of slavery. We know, from our earlier studies, of its introduction in America in 1619; let us now briefly trace its growth. From the natural differences between the northern and southern parts of the United States, the two sections came to hold very different views on the subject. We must now see the views of both, and why each held the view it did. First, as to the North. The negro slave, being held in the most complete ignorance, was fit for no kind of labor except that which he could do with his hands. This was not the kind of work in the main the North had to do. We have already seen that the soil of the North (or what was the settled North) was fairly well suited for farming; but instead of large farms, they were moderate in size, and the crops, especially in New England, had to be frequently rotated, which required intelligent supervision and care. Other laborers, except farmers, were largely engaged in manufacturing and trade, and it requires education to successfully carry on both of these kinds of labor. Thus it came about that the uneducated negro could be used to little profit in the North. This, together with the fact that the North, on account of her small farms and many kinds of labor, could not have great gangs of slaves working under one overseer, were the chief reasons why the North had few slaves, and by the close of the eighteenth century began to want to get rid of what she had. Also, some people were coming to think it was morally wrong to enslave men and women just because they were ignorant and black. We have already seen, in our earlier work, something of the plain, hard-working, liberty-loving people of the North, with their free schools, free churches and free press. It was these things which slowly inspired them with higher ideas of justice and right and caused them to wish slavery abolished from their midst. During the last half of the eighteenth century some of the people of the North and a few of the South had been doing what they could for the freedom of the slave. When laws were passed for the Northwest Territory, called the Ordinance of 1787, it was plainly stated that slavery should not be allowed there. By the Constitution it was practically agreed to allow no more slaves to be shipped into the states from foreign countries after 1808, and it was left to the original states to decide for themselves whether or not they would continue slavery within their borders. Many were coming to dislike slavery so much that by the time of the adoption of the Constitution all of the northern states except New York and New Jersey had freed their slaves; while even in the South many states had almost if not quite stopped the slave trade with Africa and between the states.

As already said, this great movement against slavery in the North was only one of the channels in which their great ideas of freedom and progress were expanding. Freedom was also growing in the Church, for most of the states by 1820 had granted entire religious freedom in their constitutions. The free school and free press were not far behind the hunter, trapper and farmer as they moved forward on the westward march.

In the South geographical conditions were different from those of the North. There, agriculture was the principal occupation. There, great gangs of slaves tended vast plantations. The great self-reliant middle class, which constituted the backbone of the North, was largely wanting in the South, and in its place was the "poor white class," as uneducated as the negro and often more criminal. The members of this class are not to be confused with the vagrants and idlers called by the negroes "yo' white trash" after the emancipation, but they were the poor and non-slaveholding whites who were renters, mechanics and overseers. While many in the South realized that slavery was an evil, they did not see how to emancipate their slaves without ruining themselves. As tobacco, cotton and rice were the main products of the southern states, the Southerners were anxious to have slavery extended. For the cultivation of these products, large farms were needed; and as the products were hard on the soil, it was necessary to move westward to obtain new soil, in place of that worn-out. This led the southern planter with his slaves across the Appalachians, first through Alabama and Mississippi, and then across the river into Louisiana, Arkansas, Missouri and Texas.

Slaves had likewise become much more profitable in the South since 1793. Until that time, of the three products named, tobacco had been the most valuable, because rice grew only in the marshy country near the coast, and it was expensive and slow work to separate the cotton fiber from the seed, since a negro working all day could clean but a single pound. But in 1793 Whitney invented a machine called a gin (or engine) for cleaning cotton, which would clean as much in a day as a thousand negroes. From this time its cultivation rapidly increased, and it soon became the most important southern product. With its uneducated negro population, and with the little flow of money into southern industry, it was impossible for the South to grow as the North did. There was not scattered over the southern plantations a class of white children thirsting for knowledge and free schools, as there was in the shops and on the farms of the North. In the South were but few intelligent white laborers developing manufactories and trade, and building towns and cities; few towns and cities made few roads, few banks, few printing presses, few newspapers, few books and comparatively few cultivated people. Moreover, the conditions of slave life do not permit of general education and culture. Slaves were sometimes taught by the southern mistresses to read and write, and they were allowed to attend church on Sundays; still, for the most part, the slave population remained uneducated. The South thought just after the close of the War of 1812 that it might build up factories as the North had done, and it was, therefore, in favor of a tariff; but it soon found that though ignorant labor may hoe cotton and tobacco, it cannot set type, run engines or manage factories.

The condition of the slave in the South was, on the whole, a very hopeless and hard one. Grouped with many others under an overseer, he hoed the tobacco, or worked in the cotton, rice or cane field and received no more than would keep him well fed and clothed. He was considered as human property, and could be, and often was, bought and sold. He had no rights of his own and generally owned no property. His condition was probably hardest in the rice fields. Rice culture requires low wet ground which can be flooded, and which therefore becomes very unhealthy as a place of labor. There the negro worked among the swamps and insects in the malarial regions along the southern shores. In the hoeing season the slaves worked grouped abreast. The men wore broad-brimmed hats, the women, head-kerchiefs. Each carried in his mouth a stick, on the end of which was a piece of burning punk made from the heart of the oak tree; the smoke from this drove away the sand flies, which would otherwise have driven him almost wild. This condition of labor made it impossible for the South to keep pace with northern growth; and this fact was seen by some of the wiser men of the South in the early part of the nineteenth century. But the southern institutions were so rooted in slavery that the southerners generally thought that to destroy slavery would be to destroy the foundation upon which all their civilization rested. Hence the southern planter lost no opportunity to push slavery into western territory and have it carved into and admitted as slave states. By doing this he hoped to hold equal representation with the North in Congress, especially in the Senate (there being two senators from each state), and thus prevent Congress from making unfavorable laws concerning the abolition of slavery, as more and more of the people of the North were beginning to wish done. Thus, as northern states were admitted with free constitutions, the South managed to have southern states admitted with constitutions recognizing slavery. By looking at the map of the United States you will see how this was. Thus, after Vermont was admitted as a free state in 1791, Kentucky and Tennessee were admitted with slavery in 1792 and 1796 respectively. This made the slave and free states equal in power in the Senate.

So the movement westward into the Mississippi Valley went on both in the North and in the South. The result was the rapid settlement of western territories and their admission to the Union. Louisiana, being finely adapted to the growth of rice and sugar-cane, was admitted in 1812, slave; Indiana in 1816, free; Mississippi in 1817, slave; Illinois in 1818, free; Alabama in 1819, slave; Maine in 1820, free; Missouri in 1821, slave. Notice that in the admission of states the number of free and slave states remained equal. In 1820 there were twenty-two states in the Union,—eleven free and eleven slave. Notice also that the boundary between the free and slave states was the southern and western boundary of Pennsylvania to the Ohio, and then down that river to the Mississippi. With the exception of Louisiana all this territory thus far admitted was east of the Mississippi, and it had not been decided by Congress whether or not slavery should be allowed to extend beyond that boundary.

Soon after the War of 1812 many emigrants from both North and South, on account of the land being more expensive east of the Mississippi, had crossed over and settled on the Missouri River. Their number rapidly increased as travel became more easy and safe both on the rivers and on the National road which the general government was building piecemeal from year to year through the great West. In 1820 those who had settled in Missouri territory asked to be admitted into the Union as a state. As many slave-owners from the southern states had moved into this territory, they wished Missouri to be admitted as a slave state; but the North, being anxious to restrict the growth of slavery, thought if it were possible to prevent slavery from moving west of the Mississippi, it might be possible at a later date to do away with it in the entire Union. The struggle which arose in Congress was a sharp one, the South being determined to carry slavery west of the Mississippi; for since Maine, in 1820, desired to enter the Union as a free state, the South felt that it was necessary to have Missouri admitted as a slave state in order that she might hold equal power with the North in the Senate. Thus you see the United States was rapidly becoming divided into two sections—one with its institutions based on slavery, the other with its institutions as firmly rooted in freedom. After much debate a compromise was agreed upon, which provided that Missouri should be admitted as a slave state, but that ever afterward all states formed from the Louisiana territory lying north of 36° 30´ north latitude should be free. This was called the Missouri Compromise, and its chief supporter was Henry Clay, who was a member of the House of Representatives from the State of Kentucky.

The slavery question in the new states now rested for near a quarter of a century, and tariff and the building of roads by the general government became the leading questions in the next administration. This was the administration of John Q. Adams, who was elected by the National Republican party in 1825 and served to 1829. The Federalist party, having become ashamed of its unwillingness to support the general government during the War of 1812, had dropped its name, but kept the old principles of a strong central government, advocating a protective tariff, a United States Bank, and internal improvements by the national government. It called itself "National Republican" till about 1832, and then took the name "Whig," which it held till it took the name "Republican party" in 1856. The strongest opponent of Adams was Jackson, the hero of New Orleans. Jackson was a supporter of the principles of Jefferson, but he was especially the leader of the new self-reliant spirit which was now rapidly growing up in the West.

In the last year of Adams' administration a tariff bill was passed, which to the South seemed very unjust, as they had now come to see that their dream of developing manufactures could not be realized. Five southern legislatures protested against the tariff law, and South Carolina threatened to disobey it, holding strongly to the idea of the right of a state to withdraw from the Union if the general government passed a law which the state thought contrary to the Constitution, which requires uniform duties throughout the United States. They looked for relief to the new President. This was Jackson, who was elected for two terms (1829–1837). But the South did not find the hoped for relief. Although the new Congress did, by separate bills, reduce the tariff in the bill of 1828, still a protective tariff was retained which the South, and especially South Carolina, considered very unjust, as it greatly aided the manufacturing North while it bore heavily on the agricultural South.

Led by her great states' rights defender, John C. Calhoun, who was at the time a United States senator, South Carolina refused to obey the tariff law. It was declared of no effect in that state in 1832. This was nullification. It meant that those who believed in states' rights held that whether or not Congress had a right to pass any given law was to be decided by each individual state; and if a state concluded that Congress was exercising power not given it in the Constitution, it might nullify the law,—that is, refuse to obey it. But the President took prompt steps to prevent nullification and to enforce the law. Congress gave him the power to do this in what was called the Force Bill; and, at the same time, through the efforts of Henry Clay, passed a compromise tariff bill. South Carolina greatly disliked the Force Bill, but, in response to the compromise tariff measure, it repealed its Ordinance of Nullification. With this compromise the doctrine of nullification slumbered till the Civil War (1861–1865) brought it forward under the claim of the right of a state to secede from the Union.

Along with the great industrial growth of the country came means for increasing the amount of money so that business of all kinds might be more easily carried on. We have already seen how the national banking System was established by Hamilton during Washington's first term. The charter for the bank, granted in 1791 for twenty years, expired in 1811. Congress failing to recharter the bank, there was no United States banking system carried on between 1811 and 1816. But in the latter year the Republican party, which originally opposed the bank, rechartered it for another term of twenty years, with a capital stock of thirty-five million dollars. It had shown itself an excellent institution for helping forward the financial affairs of the country. But President Jackson thought it was a rich, undemocratic institution, which tended to oppress the common people and help the richer classes, and that it was badly managed. So in 1832, when a bill was passed by Congress and presented to the President, asking for a continuation of its charter, Jackson vetoed it. The deposits of the United States, that is, the money which had come to the general government chiefly through the tariff, internal revenue and sale of public lands, which had been placed in the various branches of the United States Bank, were withdrawn by the Federal authorities, and the surplus funds of the government were loaned to the states in 1837. From

1836 to 1863 there was no United States banking system. But in this period hundreds of banks, chartered by the states and having little capital, sprang up all over the country. These were often called wild-cat banks, since they sprang up like wild-cats, as it were, so quickly, often almost in the woods. They issued much paper money, which, because it had little or no gold or silver behind it, soon became practically worthless, caused business to become very unsettled, many to lose their property, and was a chief cause of the panic of 1837.

In 1821, after the great compromise which allowed slavery to cross the Mississippi and enter Missouri, people said that the slavery question in the United States was settled for all time, but about 1845 it began to come forward again. In the North many were determined never to rest until slavery was abolished from the Union. Foremost among these was William Lloyd Garrison, of Boston, who published a paper called the *Liberator*, in which he declared that slavery should be destroyed at any cost. He would have even broken up the Union to do it. Abolition societies were formed, and the sentiment for freedom grew until many petitions were presented to Congress, largely by John Q. Adams, on various phases of slavery, especially for the abolition of the slave trade in the District of Columbia, the capital of the general government.

But we must not think all of United States history consisted in debates and struggles in Congress. During these times of strife over internal improvements, banks, and slavery the United States was making great but quiet steps forward in industrial lines.

Fulton in 1807 had applied steam to running boats; in 1827 it was first applied to turning wheels on land. Much money had been spent by the general government, from the close of the War of 1812 to about 1830, in improving harbors, clearing rivers of snags, rocks and sand bars, and in building roads. With settlements in towns and cities rapidly springing up in the North, there came the need for many roads for the farmer to use in transporting his products to town and in taking back his supplies to the farm. Also the general government, as already said, built roads knowing that they would assist emigrants wishing to move westward. Many people, and especially those living in the two sections—North and South,— thought differently in regard to the justice of spending the public funds for internal improvements. Many who helped pay the money, it was said, would never see or directly use them. However, improvements in rivers, harbors and roads went on rapidly, for the government felt it must bind the people together by "ducts of sympathy" if it would develop in them one strong national feeling. Roads were built extending in every direction—northwest, west and southwest. For example, a national road was built from Cumberland, Maryland, on the Potomac, almost directly west through Wheeling, West Virginia, on the Ohio River. Thence, as population grew, on through Columbus, Ohio, Indianapolis and Terre Haute, Indiana, and finally on westward till it lost itself in the broad prairies of Illinois. It was never completed to the Mississippi, as the general government at first intended, largely for the reason that the railroad came in to take its place.

The travel on this road was very great. Besides the mail and passenger coaches, there was a never-ending stream of emigrant wagons with their household property and droves pushing into the west. In 1825 the greatest enterprise yet planned for water travel was completed. This was the Erie Canal, built by the State of New York between Lake Erie and the Hudson River. By this means a water route was opened to the Atlantic from the heart of the interior, and New York City rapidly rose to be the metropolis of the country. Pork, grain and wool poured out from the West to the East. Manufactured goods of all kinds poured in from the East to the West. These roads not only carried produce back and forth, but ideas as well, and the people of the East and West, with diverse manners and customs, were thus being rapidly woven into one nation, as a great loom weaves many threads into one immense fabric.

Three years after the completion of the Erie Canal, (1828) the first American railroad was begun. It is interesting to know that the first step in this great liberalizing work was taken by the last living signer of the Declaration of Independence, Charles Carroll, of Carrollton. In 1830 fifteen miles of track were completed. At first the coaches were drawn by horses, but very soon these were replaced by the steam engine. Railroad building now went on rapidly. By 1810 there had been twenty-three hundred miles built. Thus at last had been found a means of travel which would rapidly bind the different parts of the country together with common customs, ideas and laws. The steam road not only furnished rapid means of travel, but also a cheap way of transporting goods, books, letters and newspapers. But the influence of steam did not end here. The engine was soon applied to all kinds of stationary machinery, and manufacturing was made vastly easier and a thousand-fold more rapid. Just at this time also came the discovery of the use of anthracite coal, and with the use of coal better methods of producing and working iron. It was indeed a period of rapid growth. Soon gas was introduced for lighting, and the telegraph was invented and put in use in 1844.

But the rapid progress which the United States was making was not confined merely to inventions and to material prosperity. As the people grew wealthy they obtained leisure, and leisure in turn gave opportunity for culture, refinement and the pleasures of life. Thus with growth in business came growth in religious thought, in education, in newspapers, in libraries and in literature. Before 1845, the works of Bryant, Irving, Cooper, Emerson, Hawthorne, Longfellow, Lowell, Whittier, Holmes and Bancroft had been diffused among the people by means of the free American press and were eagerly read by all classes. Schools spread throughout the West and were greatly aided by the fact that the general government gave one thirty-sixth part of the public lands for school purposes. High schools were established, and in 1839 was begun the establishment of normal schools, for the training of common-school teachers.

It is necessary, however, to keep in mind that in the progress of the country the North came to stand mainly for literature, commerce and statesmanship, while the South stood for statesmanship and agriculture. The tendencies toward practical politics and agriculture by slaves on the part of the South, and the tendencies toward literature, free labor, diverse occupations and political speculation on the part of the North, characterized respectively the settlers from the North and the South as they migrated westward. Ocean steamships which began to cross the Atlantic successfully in 1838 brought immigrants from Europe, who were quickly conveyed into the interior by the railroad and steamboat. The shops and farms westward were rapidly being filled with self-reliant settlers from New England, Scotchmen from New York, Germans from Pennsylvania; and not only with these, but with the steady stream of English, Irish and Germans now beginning to pour in from the Old World. You can easily understand, of course, whether an Englishman or German or Irishman, coming to America with wife and children, and with a living to make by daily labor, would go to the South, where education was mainly private, there being no public school system as such, and where most of the labor was performed by slaves; or to the North, where there were free schools, free labor, cheap land and hundreds of avenues for the common man to attain wealth and comfort, and a social organization without ranks and equally open to all.

Meanwhile, the new party led by Jackson had taken the name of Democratic party, while what had been called the National Republican party was now (1832) called the Whig. Jackson had been succeeded in office by Martin Van Buren, a Democrat, who served one term (1837–1841). While he was President the country was in the very depths of a financial panic.

The next campaign, 1841, was the beginning of the political rallies and processions which have grown now to be so common. W. H. Harrison, the Whig candidate, was a plain western man, and in a way, a representative of the free jovial spirit of the backwoodsman, so the principal sight in all the processions of the campaign was a log cabin with a live raccoon on top and a barrel of cider by the door. Harrison was elected President, and John Tyler, a Democrat of Virginia, was elected Vice President. Within one month the President died and Vice President Tyler succeeded him. Tyler served one term (1841–1845), and then the Democrats elected James K. Polk, of Tennessee.

Since the Louisiana Purchase, in 1803, the American people had not enlarged the boundaries of their territory except by the acquisition of Florida from Spain in 1819. But civilization, as we have seen, had been rapidly pouring back from the Appalachians to the foot of the Rockies, and the Westerner by his expansion was heeding the words of Lowell:—

> "Be broad-backed, brown-handed, upright as your pines,
> By the scale of a hemisphere shape your designs."

Now one "design " which became most prominent in 1845 was, at least by the North, considered anything but " upright." This was the plan to acquire Texas for the purpose of extending slavery therein. If you will look at your maps, you will see that the South by this time had carved all its territory into states (Arkansas had been made out of its last remaining land in 1836); so the South felt that it must have Texas in order to extend its slave institutions and to keep up the balance of power in the Senate. Texas had been a part of Mexico since 1821, when Mexico became independent of Spain; but it was now being overrun and settled largely by emigrants from the southern states. In 1836 Texas withdrew from Mexico and declared herself an independent republic. Mexico failed to reconquer Texas, and her independence was recognized by the United States. A state constitution was adopted, allowing slavery, and the state then asked for admission to the Union. The South greatly desired to have it admitted, but the North was as strongly opposed. Mexico claimed that Texas was not an independent republic and had no right to join the United States. She also declared that if the United States admitted Texas into the Union, that act would be a just cause for war between the two countries. Notwithstanding this, Congress admitted Texas in 1845, with a constitution providing for slavery. While the Texas question was gradually growing, three more states had joined the Union,—Arkansas, as already said, in 1836, Michigan in 1837 and Florida in 1845. Florida, as we have already said, at first belonged to Spain, from whom the United States bought it in 1819 for five million dollars.

No sooner had Texas been admitted to the Union, than a further dispute arose with Mexico over the southern boundary of Texas. The United States held that the boundary between Texas and Mexico was the Rio Grande River, while Mexico claimed that Texas extended only to the Nueces. The United States army occupied the territory between these two rivers and was attacked by the Mexicans. This led to a declaration of war against Mexico by the United States in

1846. The war lasted two years, and it is generally thought to have been a very unjust war on the part of the United States against a weaker nation. Although the Mexicans put larger armies into the field than did the United States, they were defeated in every battle, until Mexico was invaded by the United States army and its capital taken.

While this was going on, United States troops seized California and New Mexico. When a treaty of peace between the two nations was signed, in 1848, Mexico gave up not only the territory between the Nueces and the Rio Grande, which was the immediate cause of the war, but, in addition to this, all Mexican territory north of the Gila River, and extending from the Rocky Mountains to the Pacific Ocean. This included New Mexico, California, Nevada, Utah, Arizona and parts of Colorado and Wyoming. But the Anglo-Saxon hunger for territory was not yet satisfied. The Americans immediately began to make plans to secure that part of America west of the Rocky Mountains and north of the forty-second parallel, called the Oregon territory. This territory was claimed by both England and the United States, and had been partly settled by both countries. The United States claimed that the northern boundary was 54° 40′, but England refused to grant this claim. For a time it looked as if there would be war between the two countries, but in the end it was settled by a treaty in which the northern boundary of the United States was fixed at the forty-ninth parallel.

Following these years of territorial growth, the United States continued to grow in improvements and inventions. By the use of the telegraph it became possible to operate large railway systems. Farming was helped greatly by the introduction of improved farm machinery: for example, the McCormick reaper, patented in 1834, soon did away with the slow method of reaping wheat with the sickle and cradle, and the steam engine which displaced horse power as a means of threshing grain did away with the flail and the winnowing of wheat by hand. Thus, while the East was manufacturing cotton and woolen goods, the West was manufacturing farms and sending its raw material rapidly eastward by means of steamboat, canal and railroad.

In 1848 gold was discovered in California. The telegraph and newspaper spread the news of the vast wealth of the Pacific coast like magic over the world, and almost immediately from all parts of the United States, from Europe and South America, came gold hunters on a mad rush through the western mountains, across the isthmus of Panama, and around Cape Horn, to California. In the year 1849 almost eighty thousand immigrants rushed into California to dig gold. In that year the new settlers drew up a constitution, excluding slavery, and asked to be admitted to the Union. There were few slave men in California, for the owners could not take slaves there and use them to great advantage in mining. Soon the same old question of slavery and freedom arose; that is, should slavery be allowed to enter this new public territory or not? The North was making great efforts in the press and in Congress to admit it free, although most of it lay south of the parallel of 36° 30′, the Missouri Compromise line, as you will remember, on the east side of the Rockies, which divided the free and slave states.

This was the leading question before the people in the campaign of 1849. It resulted in the election of Taylor, the Whig candidate, who had become famous as a general in the Mexican War. No sooner had the new administration begun, in 1850, than the slavery question was pushed rapidly to the front. From all this we can see how far the question was from being settled "forever," as the politicians had said it was when Missouri was admitted in 1821. The contest over the admission of the new western land was bitter, but it was ended for a short time in 1850 by a compromise proposed by Henry Clay, who because of his many compromise bills in Congress was called the "peacemaker." The bill proposed to settle at one and the same time all of the disputes that had grown out of the slavery contest. From its effort to make provision for settling all the great questions then dividing the South from the North it was called the Omnibus Bill. Its chief provisions were: (1) California was admitted as a free state. (2) Slave trading was stopped in the District of Columbia. (3) Utah and New Mexico were organized as territories without any mention of slavery, leaving that question to be determined by the settlers who should go therein. (4) The United States paid Texas a large sum of money for a claim held by Texas upon a portion of what is now New Mexico. (5) A Fugitive Slave Law, made very favorable for catching runaway slaves, was passed by Congress. It is thought, if President Taylor had lived the bill would not have been passed, but in 1850 he died, and Vice President Fillmore became President and signed it.

Those who voted for the Compromise Bill of 1850 thought, or at any rate desired to think, that they were quietly settling the entire slavery dispute forever. Instead of this they were throwing fuel into the flame. The advantages gained from the compromise by the South, and especially the provision concerning catching and returning fugitive slaves who had escaped from them, only made many people of the North more determined to resist the further growth of slavery, and if possible utterly to destroy it. This was shown when slave owners from the South, acting under the Fugitive Slave Law, tried to arrest escaped negroes in the northern states and take them back South. Sympathy for the negroes in the northern states had grown so strong that many persons sheltered runaway slaves and helped them to escape. Routes were established by which fugitives were taken forward, often during the night-time, from station to station, into Canada. These routes were called under-ground railroads, because by them it was possible to assist the negro northward so quickly and secretly. Of course this made the South very angry with the North, and much the same feeling was held by the North toward the South. The North and South, as we have already seen, had never been genuinely and closely united. In schools, education, systems of labor, government and social opportunities it is easy to see that the two sections were drifting farther and farther apart.

In 1854 a bill was presented to Congress for the organization of Nebraska, which was to include all the territory of the Louisiana Purchase north of the line of the Missouri Compromise (36° 30′) and west of the states of Iowa and Missouri. Finally the bill was changed, and provided that the territory should be divided into two territories, (1) Kansas just west of Missouri and (2) Nebraska west of Iowa. The bill also declared that the slavery provision of the Missouri Compromise had been done away with by the provision of 1850 concerning Utah and New Mexico, which, as you remember, left it to the settlers of those two territories to decide whether they would have freedom or slavery when they asked for admission as states into the Union. Since this privilege had been granted to those two territories, the South, led by Stephen A. Douglas of Illinois, argued that the same privilege ought to be granted to all territories formed by the general government. This argument prevailed in Congress, and the Kansas-Nebraska Bill passed (1854), granting the right to the people who settled in those territories to decide for themselves whether they would or would not have slaves brought in and settled among them. The passing of this bill was thought to be another great victory for the South. It placed power in the hands of the state government which had heretofore been exercised by the general government, namely, that of determining whether any given territory entering the Union should have slavery in it or not. When the bill passed, two streams of settlers—a northern and a southern—immediately set out from the eastern states toward Kansas. Slave owners, taking with them slaves and many rude, shiftless people from the South, were first on the ground. The North likewise was determined to get possession of the state.

Emigration societies were formed in eastern cities, by means of which money was raised and northern settlers hurried into the territory. Very soon trouble arose between the different peoples settling there, and for some time Kansas was a scene of bloody struggle between the northern and southern settlers. The war between slavery and freedom had really begun. This was during the administration of Franklin Pierce, a Democrat, who succeeded Fillmore in 1853. The slavery party proved at first strongest in Kansas, but the constitution formed by this party was refused by Congress, when Kansas asked for admission, because it had been voted upon unlawfully by the border ruffians of Missouri and other southern states, who crossed over into the territory temporarily for the purpose of carrying the election for slavery. The result was that Kansas remained a territory until 1861, and then entered the Union as a free state after the southern members had withdrawn from Congress. This was the last hope of the South for securing slave territory in the West. The forces of freedom were growing stronger every day, and the South saw that finally she would certainly be overwhelmed by them. What she finally concluded to do to save her institution of slavery, we shall presently see.

In 1857 James Buchanan was elected President by the Democratic party. This year was also marked by an important decision of the Supreme Court. A negro, named Dred Scott, who was the slave of a surgeon in the regular army, living in the state of Missouri, had been taken by his owner into Illinois, a free state, then to the northern part of the Louisiana Purchase (in what is now Minnesota), where slavery was "forever prohibited" by the Missouri Compromise, and finally was taken back to Missouri, a slave state. Being whipped by his master, Scott sued for his freedom, claiming that having lived in a free state and a free territory, he had become a free man. The Supreme Court of the United States decided against him,—that is, it decided that taking a slave into a free state did not make him any less a slave. The effect of this decision on the North was very great. The people saw that it gave the slave owners right to over-run their free territory with slaves. It practically threw the North open, temporarily at least, to the slave holders of the South, and it made the North only the more determined to destroy slavery. Abolition literature was printed in the northern states and sent broadcast over the country, especially in the South, and greater efforts were made to aid escaping slaves. A new man now entered the slavery contest. This was Abraham Lincoln,—a man like Socrates, Luther and Franklin, of plain, simple and natural manner, who had not been educated in schools and universities, but had "mixed with action" in the great Practical University of Life, and, knowing the hopes and struggles of the common people, came to love and believe in them. He saw that the settlement of the slavery problem could not be put off much longer. Slave uprisings were becoming more and more common in the South. In the North negro schools were sometimes established. In 1859 John Brown tried to arouse the slaves in Virginia to rebel by seizing the United States Arsenal at Harper's Ferry, Virginia, and arming the slaves, but this brave man was soon captured and hanged for treason. But still the spirit of liberty for which he stood went "marching on," for there was growing to be a vast number in the North who saw, as Lincoln said, that our nation could not long remain "half slave and half free." "A house divided against itself," he said, "cannot stand." Lincoln became the leader of the northern sentiment, and the presidential candidate, in 1860, of the Republican party, to which the Whig party had now changed its name. Although the platform of 1860, upon which he was elected, expressly declared that the Republican Party merely intended to prevent slavery from extending any farther into public territory than it had already done, Lincoln believed and said in his speeches not long before this time that the state of affairs then existing could not permanently last; that slavery must extend to all the states or be entirely destroyed. "I believe," he said in a great speech in 1858, "that this government cannot endure half slave and half free. I do not expect the Union to be dissolved—I do not expect the house to fall—but I do expect it will cease to be divided. It will become all one thing or all the other." When Lincoln became President, in 1861, he said: "I have no purpose, directly or indirectly, to interfere with the institution of slavery in the states where it exists. I believe I have no lawful right to do so, and I have no inclination to do so." Nevertheless, the South thought that his election meant their ruin, for that was, they thought, what the loss of their slaves meant. South Carolina, always quickest to defend what she regarded as her rights, took the lead of the southern states and determined to withdraw from the Union.

Before going farther let us take a brief view of the condition of the country in general, both North and South. Between 1850 and 1861 five new states had been admitted—Iowa in 1846, Wisconsin in 1848, Minnesota in 1858, Oregon in 1859, Kansas 1861, all free. The population of the country had now grown to be over thirty-one million. Emigration, mostly belonging to the middle class, had pushed rapidly forward to the middle and western states; but practically none had gone to the South. The South was rich in soil, with some stores of coal and iron and vast fields of cane, cotton and tobacco, but fully one-third of the population were slaves. Slavery had destroyed the middle class and had made a "poor white class" as far below "the planter" as the serf of the Middle Ages was below his lord. The North had many large cities teeming with wealth, bound together by railroads and telegraph lines. Steam had been put to turning the wheels of the printing press, and with books, magazines and newspapers, America was in the midst of the "golden age" of her literature. Prescott and Motley wrote histories which attracted the whole world; Bryant, amid his labors as journalist, struck off his undying poems; Longfellow told the tale of love which recalled our ancestral connection with Plymouth and the *Mayflower.* Whittier sang the songs of freedom; Lowell, Holmes and Curtis, in the purest of English, addressed millions of readers through *Harper's*, *Putnam's* and *The Atlantic*, and Emerson spoke such words of wisdom and inspiration that they cannot be classed as belonging to any particular age. It was a day when opportunities were expanding; when *the common man* was beginning to count in schemes of government, industry and education. In fact, the North was rapidly becoming a government "of the people, by the people, and for the people"; while the South, although recognizing the rights of the "poor whites," and often treating the slaves humanely, was essentially and with great ability a government of the slaveholders, by the slaveholders, and for the slaveholders.

On the twentieth day of December, 1860, South Carolina, in convention called for that purpose, declared (1) That she had a right to abolish a government seeking to rule her, which, in her opinion, had become destructive of the ends for which it was set up; (2) that the non-slaveholding states had broken the Constitution by passing laws protecting slaves who had run away from their masters and escaped to the North, that, therefore, South Carolina was released from her obligations to abide by the Constitution; and (3) that as a sovereign state she had a right to govern herself, and for the reasons already stated, she would withdraw from the Union. Before March, 1861, six other states had joined South Carolina. Those states were Mississippi, Florida, Alabama, Georgia, Louisiana and Texas. Later Virginia, North Carolina, Tennessee and Arkansas joined them, making in all eleven. They formed a Confederacy, known as the Confederate States of America. They selected Richmond, Virginia, as the Confederate capital, and chose Jefferson Davis President and Alexander H. Stephens Vice President. They seized all Federal government property within their limits and prepared to defend themselves against any move the North might make. They thought they had a right to withdraw from the Union, and felt sure of success in any contest with the North. They had lost control of the central government in Congress, and seceded because: (1) they saw that the North would not consent to further slavery extension; (2) because the northern states were assisting their slaves to escape (which was a violation of Art. 4, § 2, cl. 3, of the Constitution); and (3) because they thought that President Lincoln intended to destroy slavery wherever it existed in the United States. Although he did not intend to do this, and, as we have seen, expressly declared that he did not, he had sworn to protect the Union and preserve it. This he intended to do, at whatever cost. "I shall take care," he said in his first inaugural address, "as the Constitution itself expressly enjoins upon me, that the laws of the Union be faithfully executed in all the states." Lincoln was a western man, who was reared when a child in a log-cabin in Kentucky. At seven years of age he moved with his parents from Kentucky to Indiana, and at the age of twenty-one from Indiana to the wilderness of Illinois. He rose by his own efforts to be as great a statesman as Washington and one of the greatest in the history of the world. Being a plain man himself, he had profound confidence in the plain people. He said of them, "You can fool all the people some of the time, some of the people all of the time, but you can't fool all the people all the time." In dealing with the slavery question, he followed a cautious but straightforward policy, moving no faster than he could carry the people with him. A like straightforward and just policy was followed also by the President in dealing with the seceded states. He at once declared that the southern states were in rebellion against the Union and called for volunteers to compel them to remain peaceably in the Union. Both sides began all preparations for the great struggle. We can see at a moment's thought which side was the stronger and better prepared for war. It requires money, men, arms, and a great cause to fight for, to make a great war. The North had more men, more money and more arms, more free schools, free governments and *free men* than the South, and until the Emancipation Proclamation, January, 1863, had the great principle of *the Union* ("half slave and half free") to fight for. After the Emancipation Proclamation, till April, 1865, a vastly greater principle to fight for, namely, a Union based upon the immortal principle of the Declaration of Independence, that "All men are created equal," and should have the inalienable right to pursue life, liberty and happiness unhindered. The South too felt that it was fighting for a great cause when it fought to maintain the principle that each state, being its own judge, should have the right wholly to rule itself in case the general government treated it unjustly, and in defense of its property right in slaves as guaranteed by the Constitution. The principle of local self-government is a precious one to all Anglo-Saxon Americans. It was born two thousand years ago with the Teutonic race in the German forests, and it has grown ever stronger as that race has increased in strength, and conquered the fairest parts of the earth. That it did not prevail in the war from 1861 to 1865 to the extent of dismembering the Union, all sections of our harmonious Republic now equally rejoice. What the South lacked in arms, money and men it made up for in a struggle so brave that its courage was only equaled by that of the North, and its self-sacrifice was in every way equal to its courage. Moreover, no other war in all history, perhaps, involving such great personal sacrifice, can show those who were defeated as having accepted the results of the conflict in as fine a spirit or with as true a patriotism as those have who fought on the Confederate side in the late struggle between the northern and southern states.

This struggle, called the War of the Rebellion, or the Civil War, lasted four years. We cannot follow it in detail. At first the southern arms were mainly successful, but the swelling tide of liberty in the North soon began to overcome them. They had neither the men nor means to keep up the struggle. Their downfall was hastened when, on January 1, 1863, having felt that the people at home and the nations abroad were ready for it, and that it was a necessary means of saving the Union, Lincoln issued the Emancipation Proclamation, proclaiming all the slaves in the states then in rebellion free. Without their slaves to cultivate their land and thus furnish means with which to carry on the war, the South could not hold out long. Although urged by some to proclaim the slaves free at the beginning of the war, Lincoln declared he had no intention of doing so unless the life of the Union required it. He finally made the proclamation as a means of weakening the South, ending the war and saving the Union. His power to do this was disputed, but in 1865 Congress proposed an Amendment to the Constitution, which was ratified by the states, abolishing slavery entirely from the United States. As already said, the southern states were overcome by larger armies, and finally, when the South was bankrupt and in ruins, when they had suffered as probably no other people in modern times have suffered, the South gave up the struggle, and General Lee surrendered his army to General Grant at Appomattox Courthouse, Virginia, on April 9, 1865. The first act of Grant in dealing with Lee's surrendered and starving army was calculated to heal the great breach between the two great sections. He issued food to the starving men and sent them back home with their horses, saying, they would need them for the spring plowing. Lincoln and Grant, supported by the free *common men* of the nation, had thus saved the Union which it cost Washington and the Revolutionary patriots so much sacrifice to create. But in addition to the cost of money and men it cost the life of the great Lincoln. On April 14, 1865, he was shot, while attending the theater in Washington, by John Wilkes Booth, a southern sympathizer. Immediately the rejoicing in the North over peace and victory was turned into universal grief. The death of the great man who had guided the Nation through the storm was felt as an irreparable loss by the South as well as the North, and it moved the sympathy of the entire world. Lincoln was succeeded in office by Andrew Johnson, the Vice President, on whom fell the great task of restoring the South from the effects of secession and war and of cementing the states into one harmonious Union.

What were the results of the war? Since the formation of the Union many had believed in the right of nullification and ultimately of the right of secession on the part of a state. This question was now settled forever. The war proved (1) that ours is a Union in which there can be no secession. No state can withdraw from the Union, nor can the Union interfere with the rights of the states. Then (2) slavery was destroyed forever. To sum it up briefly, it may be said that the war proved that the United States is an indestructible, Federal Union made up of indestructible states, wherein slavery shall not exist but where every one shall be free to make the most and best possible of himself. The war thus saved for posterity the example of a nation based upon the great principles worked out by the greatest peoples of the past. It saved the Roman principle of a strong central government; it united with this the Teutonic principle of a strong local government; it may be truly said to have saved the Greek principles of art and philosophy by making it possible for everybody to enter freely into school and university and gain that culture upon which these are based. In short, the war saved a nation, based upon the oldest, broadest and most abiding principle of humanity,—human freedom. It made America, as Emerson said, another word for opportunity. Much trouble was had in rebuilding the Union, but slowly the southern states came back to their former standing. Since the close of the Civil War, the negro, by constitutional amendments, has been made a citizen and been given the right to vote and all rights of American citizenship; but the past injustice to that race imposes on America a great duty to assist the negro in the future to lift himself up to the blessings of civilization. Time has taken away the feeling of bitterness between the North and South, and the country now is united as never before. Since the negro has been freed, the South itself has awakened to a new life. It has grown greatly in wealth and learning, and finds free labor more profitable than formerly it found slave. The country is still directed politically by two main political parties,—the Democratic, holding essentially to the principle of local government, upon which it was founded by Jefferson; and the Republican, holding to the principle of strong national government, the principle upon which it was founded by Hamilton, Washington, Adams and Jay. Many other important questions still face the people of the United States and call for the greatest wisdom in their settlement. The means of securing honest, capable officers for carrying on the government,—national, state, municipal,—the best means of regulating trusts, the best means of securing to the daily laborer a just reward for his labor, demand as great statesmanship for settlement as did the bank, tariff, internal improvements, and slavery questions, which were the great political issues during the first three-quarters of our national life.

Moreover, in 1898 America was for a time at war with Spain for the freedom of Cuba. In this war the United States was again successful, and among its many effects it brought the North and South closer together in friendship, perhaps, than they had ever been since the formation of the Union. In this war the Philippine Islands, Cuba and Porto Rico were taken from Spain, and a great question of that time was how the United States could best discharge its duties toward these foreign possessions. In dealing thus far with these outlying territories, our country has acted with promptness and energy; for, after spending millions of dollars in freeing Cuba, establishing an admirable school system therein, providing for popular elections, establishing hospitals and charitable institutions, cleaning and reorganizing the prisons, introducing sanitation, thus making one of the most unhealthy countries of the world one of comparative healthfulness, the United States, on May 27, 1902, of its own accord (one of the most honorable acts in the history of the world) lowered its own flag, raised the Cuban emblem of national independence in its place and bade God-speed to the new republic which it had liberated, nourished and launched into independent life. Thus, you see, while we do not have the same struggles to make, in settlement of exactly the same questions that our forefathers had, we have as great and as important ones. And the main purpose of all the study we have given to the development of history throughout all the ages has been to see how the great principles of human liberty have been fought for, won and developed, and how they have sometimes been lost through carelessness, ignorance and selfishness. All along the track of time, for thousands of years, people have been sacrificing, and giving the things most precious to them,—even to their lives,—that men and women and children might be free to make the very most and best of their lives of which they are capable. In order to obtain the value that historical study should give, one must catch the spirit of justice, kindness and helpfulness, and highly resolve to work with might in some avenue which will better mankind. He who truly studies Greece or the Renaissance will seek to bring beauty to schoolroom and home by putting picture and library and beauty and culture within them. He who truly studies the best that Rome achieved in her thousand years of history will gradually feel the great virtues of perseverance, obedience to authority and patriotism which Rome taught, etching their way into his character. He who follows the growth of religion through its hundreds of generations, and Christianity through its centuries of development and sees the growth of the universal Church from age to age, ever catching new truth and broader views, will come to see the good which has been, and is being accomplished by every religion, creed and profession. Out of such views toleration will arise, narrowness and bigotry will disappear, and the hand of sympathy and helpfulness will be reached forth not alone to kindred and neighbors and countrymen and fellow-Christians but to fellow-men

> "Where'er a human spirit strives
> After a life more true and fair."

He who truly studies the history of America will come to see and feel that the great principles of freedom which we enjoy have their roots lying deep in the past,—that all great nations and great men have given their noblest efforts and their lives to establish and advance these principles; that the truest patriotism and service to country, therefore, does not consist in a narrow and slavish subservience to party, creed, or country, but in an earnest and intelligent effort to see the truth which exists in every party, creed and nation, and in a life devoted to advancing the immortal principles of human liberty upon which our government is based and which all ages and all nations have contributed in some degree to bequeath to us. It is by some such conception of patriotism and true love of country as this that the student of history becomes broad, liberal, many-sided,—a true interpreter of the past, a safe guide for the present and a guarantee to the future "that government of the people, by the people, and for the people, shall not perish from the earth."

CPSIA information can be obtained at www.ICGtesting.com
Printed in the USA
BVOW08s1145010716

454228BV00001B/14/P

9 781599 152608